Women Who Win

Laila Ali

Cynthia Cooper

Lindsay Davenport

Mia Hamm

Martina Hingis

Chamique Holdsclaw

Marion Jones

Anna Kournikova

Michelle Kwan

Lisa Leslie

Gabrielle Reece

Dorothy "Dot" Richardson

Sheryl Swoopes

Venus & Serena Williams

CHELSEA HOUSE PUBLISHERS

WOMEN WHO WIN

Gabrielle Reece

Dynise Balcavage

Introduction by
HANNAH STORM

CHELSEA HOUSE PUBLISHERS
Philadelphia

Frontis: Through hard work and perseverance, Gabby was able to break down the wall between beauty and athleticism, showing both the sports and fashion worlds that the two ideals could coexist.

ACKNOWLEDGEMENTS
Many thanks to Jane Kachmer, Gabrielle Reece's agent, for all of her help.

CHELSEA HOUSE PUBLISHERS

Editor in Chief: Sally Cheney
Director of Production: Kim Shinners
Production Manager: Pamela Loos
Art Director: Sara Davis
Production Editor: Diann Grasse

Staff for Gabrielle Reece
Editor: Sally Cheney
Associate Editor: Benjamin Kim
Associate Art Director: Takeshi Takahashi
Layout by D&G Limited.

The Chelsea House World Wide Web address is
http://www.chelseahouse.com

First Printing

1 3 5 7 9 8 6 4 2

Library of Congress Cataloging-in-Publication Data

Balcavage, Dynise.
  Gabrielle Reece / Dynise Balcavage.
    p. cm. – (Women who win)
Includes bibliographical references (p.) and index.
ISBN 0-7910-6531-6 (alk. paper)
  1. Reece, Gabrielle—Juvenile literature 2. Volleyball players —United
  States—Biography—Juvenile literature. 3. Women volleyball players—
  United States—Biography—Juvenile literature. [1. Reece, Gabrielle.
  2. Volleyball players. 3. Women—Biography.] I. Title. II. Series.

GV1015.26.R44 B35 2001
796.325'092—dc21
[B]   2001028907

Contents

WOMEN WHO WIN

Hannah Storm
NBC Studio Host

Y̲ou go girl! Women's sports are the hottest thing going right now, with the 1900s ending in a big way. When the U.S. team won the 1999 Women's World Cup, it captured the imagination of all sports fans and served as a great inspiration for young girls everywhere to follow their dreams.

That was just the exclamation point on an explosive decade for women's sports—capped off by the Olympic gold medals for the U.S. women in hockey, softball, and basketball. All the excitement created by the U.S. national basketball team helped to launch the Women's National Basketball Association (WNBA), which began play in 1997. The fans embraced the concept, and for the first time, a successful and stable women's professional basketball league was formed.

I was the first ever play-by-play announcer for the WNBA—a big personal challenge. Broadcasting, just like sports, had some areas with limited opportunities for women. There have traditionally not been many play-by-play opportunities for women in sports television, so I had no experience. To tell you the truth, the challenge I faced was a little scary! Sometimes we are all afraid that we might not be up to a certain task. It is not easy to take risks, but unless we push ourselves we will stagnate and not grow.

Here's what happened to me. I had always wanted to do play-by-play earlier in my career, but I had never gotten the opportunity. Not that I was unhappy—I had been given studio hosting assignments that were unprecedented for a woman and my reputation was well established in the business. I was comfortable in my role . . . plus I had just had my first baby. The last thing I needed to do was suddenly tackle a new skill on national television and risk being criticized (not to mention, very stressed out!). Although I had always wanted to do play-by-play, I turned down the assignment twice, before reluctantly agreeing to give it a try. During my hosting stint of the NBA finals that year, I traveled back and forth to WNBA preseason games to practice play-by-play. I was on 11 flights in 14 days to seven different cities! My head was spinning and it was no surprise that I got sick. On the day of the first broadcast, I had to have shots just so I could go on the air without throwing up. I felt terrible and nervous, but I survived my first game. I wasn't very good but gradually, week by week,

I got better. By the end of the season, the TV reviews of my work were much better—*USA Today* called me "most improved."

During that 1997 season, I witnessed a lot of exciting basketball moments, from the first historic game to the first championship, won by the Houston Comets. The challenge of doing play-by-play was really exciting and I loved interviewing the women athletes and seeing the fans' enthusiasm. Over one million fans came to the games; my favorite sight was seeing young boys wearing the jerseys of female players—pretty cool. And to think I almost missed out on all of that. It reinforced the importance of taking chances and not being afraid of challenges or criticism. When we have an opportunity to follow our dreams, we need to go for it!

Thankfully, there are now more opportunities than ever for women in sports (and other areas, like broadcasting). We thank women, like those in this series, who have persevered despite lack of opportunities—women who have refused to see their limitations. Remember, women's sports has been around a long time. Way back in 396 B.C. Kyniska, a Spartan princess, won an Olympic chariot race. Of course, women weren't allowed to compete, so she was not allowed to collect her prize in person. At the 1996 Olympic games in Atlanta, Georgia, over 35,600 women competed, almost a third more than in the previous Summer Games. More than 20 new women's events have been added for the Sydney, Australia, Olympics in 2000. Women's collegiate sports continues to grow,spurred by the 1972 landmark legislation Title IX, which states that "no person in the United States shall, on the basis of sex, be excluded from participation in, be denied the benefits of, or be subjected to discrimination under any educational program or activity receiving federal financial assistance." This has set the stage for many more scholarships and opportunities for women, and now we have professional leagues as well. No longer do the most talented basketball players in the country have to go to Europe or Asia to earn a living.

The women in this series did not have as many opportunities as you have today. But they were persistent through all obstacles, both on the court and off. I can tell you that Cynthia Cooper is the strongest woman I know. What is it that makes Cynthia and the rest of the women included in this series so special? They are not afraid to share their struggles and their stories with us. Their willingness to show us their emotions, open their hearts, bare their souls, and let us into their lives is what, in my mind, separates them from their male counterparts. So accept this gift of their remarkable stories and be inspired. Because you, too, have what it takes to follow your dreams.

1

MOST IMPROVED PLAYER

Standing 6 feet, 3 inches, Gabrielle Reece was the tallest woman to ever play volleyball for Florida State University's (FSU) Lady Seminoles. Gabby, as everyone called her, enjoyed the sport. She had even won a scholarship to play at FSU. Even though she was a talented athlete, she was not the team's best player. In fact, Gabby had nervously watched her team's first seven games from the bench.

Gabby's coach, Cecile Reynaud, knew the freshman's game needed work. In order to motivate her to improve, she pushed Gabby much harder than her teammates, often ordering Gabby to serve 10 balls into the middle of the court. If one ball landed short, the rest of the team would have to run a drill, called a "suicide," as punishment. Partly because of Coach Reynaud's clever coaching technique, Gabby felt a great deal of pressure to play better.

In 1994, Gabrielle's looks and talent attracted the attention of Nike footwear, who signed her to a lucrative contract to promote their products. Here, she jumps rope during a Nike photo shoot. Gabby's natural beauty and aggressive style of play proved a winning combination for Nike.

By the eighth game of the season, she was finally ready to play in a match. Despite the fact that she had natural athletic talent and was tall enough to easily block and outmaneuver her opponents, Gabby was not exactly looking forward to participating. Although she had practiced hard and had studied her teammates' moves from the bench, she did not feel confident.

When a ball lands within a volleyball player's reach, they usually yell out "Me! Me! Me!" to tell their teammates that they want to hit it. But Gabby secretly hoped she would not have to hit the ball. "I was saying to myself, 'please, anyone but me,'" she later explained in her book *Big Girl in the Middle.*

But she soon became accustomed to the pressures of practice and competition. Positioned as middle hitter, Gabby learned the finer points of blocking the ball—jumping up against the net and stopping the opponent's ball from crossing to her team's side of the court. She also got quite good at making "kills"—scoring points by hitting the ball so hard that it lands on the other team's side of the court before they can hit it.

By the end of the 1987 season, the Lady Seminoles had achieved a proud record of 22 wins and 11 losses. The team even advanced far enough to play in the National Collegiate Athletic Association (NCAA) tournament. Unfortunately, the team was knocked out in the very first round, but Gabby ended up a winner. Her season record included 175 blocks and 178 kills. The girl who had been so afraid to play was voted the team's Most Improved Player.

Already a successful model and athlete, in 1997 Gabby co-authored *Big Girl in the Middle*, an autobiographical book of her life and experiences on the court.

Around the same time, Gabby was strolling around the FSU campus when she caught the eye of a fashion scout. When she was younger, her mother had taken her to a modeling school, but they told her Gabby was too tall to model. By this time, however, the fashion world's tastes had changed. Now, tall models were "in." Gabby's height, chiseled features, full lips, and graceful neck and shoulders impressed the scout, who encouraged her to model.

Gabby nervously told Coach Reynaud about the opportunity. She expected her to be angry, or at least upset. Much to Gabby's surprise, Coach Reynaud stood behind her decision to give modeling a try. She even gave her some good advice. "When you are here, you are here," she told Gabby. "When you are there, you are there."

So when the semester ended in June, Gabby flew to New York to embark on yet another new adventure. For a while, she stayed with Aunt Norette and Uncle Joe, the couple who had raised her from ages three to seven. Thanks to financial help from Uncle Joe, Gabby was able to rent a small apartment in Manhattan, New York, one of the capitals of the fashion world.

Once settled, Gabby signed with IMG Modeling Agency, earning $3,500 for her first job as a hand model for Cutex, a nail polish company. Strangely, for this particular photo shoot, neither her height nor good looks came into play. Gabby thought the photo shoot was a bit ironic as well, because volleyball players do not usually have nice hands. Their skin often gets bruised and calloused from the long hours practicing. Hand models, however, take extra special care of their hands. They usually avoid any rough activities and even wear protective gloves. But Gabby's hands worked out well for the assignment, and she was happy with the money she had earned.

Gabby's next job turned out to be a ground-breaking one. Her agency flew her to Italy. She was scheduled to do a photo shoot for Italian Vogue—one of the world's best-known fashion magazines. One of the industry's most respected fashion photographers, Stephen Meisel, was scheduled to take the photos. Gabby turned out to be natural in front of the camera, comfortable posing and being photographed. The resulting shots showed a confident, self-assured woman.

Meisel's masterpieces appeared on the magazine's cover and in an eight-page spread within the magazine. Meisel used strong contrasts and shadows to show off Gabby's pouty lips, strong chin, mysterious eyes, and athletic physique.

Although this glamorous stint impressed many people, Gabby did not take the modeling too seriously. She was glad to have the opportunity. But even though she was only 19, she proved to be wise for her years. She knew how fickle the fashion world could be.

"I never stopped and thought, 'Isn't this great?' For me, for my personality, it's a waste of emotion," she said. "And I'm not going to waste my emotion on transient things—they're there, then they're gone . . . I could never let my existence rely on that."

That summer, Gabby earned a lot of money modeling and traveled to many exotic places.

Even though she could have easily quit college to earn a lucrative living as a model, the thought of giving up volleyball, the sport she had grown to love, never crossed her mind. She did not think twice about returning to FSU. By the end of the summer, she was back on the court practicing.

Since the NCAA's rules stated that scholarship students were not allowed to work, Gabby had to give up her athletic scholarship. But because of her modeling earnings, this did not cause much of a problem. She also used some of the money to purchase her own house— quite an adult decision for a 19-year-old.

"I wanted roots that badly," she remembered. "But I wasn't really enjoying anything. I was so busy trying to be grown-up and serious, I didn't understand that being grown-up does-n't mean being serious, it just means making sure your bills are paid."

Because her mom had left her on her own so often, Gabby became what psychologists call a "parental child." She had spent her entire childhood behaving like an adult, making adult decisions, and taking on adult responsibilities. Now, at 19, she *was* an adult, and she making responsible decisions to prove it. She was earning her own living, working long hours practicing her volleyball game, and studying.

Gabby's remarkable sense of responsibility, combined with her talent, intelligence, and a few healthy doses of good luck, set the stage for her two future careers. Even though she seemed to make all the right decisions and, like a cat, to always land on her feet, success did not come without its price.

2

A LIFE ON THE MOVE

During the 1970s, many people—mostly teenagers and college students—were disgusted by the lives lost during the Vietnam War. Instead of war, these young people believed in peace, love, nature, and freedom of expression. They were called "hippies."

With her flowing blonde locks, Terry Glynn looked like a typical hippie girl. Born on Long Island, New York, she was a free spirit who searched for things and people that made her happy. In 1969 in San Diego, California, Terry met Robert "Bobby" Eduardo Reece. He came from a prominent family from the Caribbean island of Trinidad. He was earning an advanced degree in human behavior at the United States International University.

Soon, Terry and Bobby fell in love. They were both stunningly good-looking and made a striking pair. Terry's honey blonde hair, amazing height and high cheekbones turned many heads. Bobby was a tall, dark, and handsome man with exotic features. He stood six feet tall—two inches shorter than Terry. His sea-green eyes were framed by black, thick lashes. The couple married, and on January 6, 1970, their daughter, Gabrielle, was born in

While representing Team Nike on the court, Gabby still had time to design a sneaker of her own and land a gig as a correspondent for *MTV Sports*, a TV program profiling pro athletes.

LaJolla, California. She inherited her mother's height and her father's piercing green eyes.

Gabby, as she was called, was a pretty, chubby-cheeked baby. Childhood pictures show a towheaded, contented toddler, walking with her parents on the beach and cuddling with her dad. Unfortunately, Terry and Bobby's romance did not last. When Gabby was just two years old, the couple separated.

Terry loved the water and often swam for two hours at a time. When she landed a job in Mexico City training dolphins for a circus, it seemed like the perfect opportunity to combine a career with her love for the water. The circus even used Terry's picture for one of its promotional posters. She took young Gabby with her.

But Gabby did not fare as well in Mexico as her mother. She developed a nasty, hacking cough. When her daughter did not get any better, Terry became worried and took Gabby see a doctor. The doctor said the child had whooping cough.

Mexico City was a very polluted place, and Terry thought that the dirty air was making her daughter sick. She decided that Gabby's health would improve if she lived where the air was cleaner, so she took her to Long Island, New York. Gabby was to stay with Terry's friends and childhood neighbors, Norette and Joe Zucarello, in their small house. After a brief visit, Terry left without her young daughter.

Sweethearts since age 15, the Zucarellos had no children of their own. They were thrilled to have the perky little blonde in their lives, even though they knew it would not be for long. From the way Terry had been talking, they expected her to return to pick up Gabby in just a few weeks.

Meanwhile, the Zucarellos bought a white Samoyed dog to keep their young guest company. Gabby originally was going to name the dog Ballerina, but then changed her mind and named her Daisy.

The weeks with the Zucarellos melted into months. One day when she was three and a half, Gabby was sitting in her room, looking at the glitzy promotional poster of Terry posing with the dolphins and suddenly realized that her mom was not coming back. She ripped down the poster and replaced it with a big picture of Elvis Presley.

Although she missed her mom, the fact that Gabby's life was filled with love and activities helped her feel less lonely. She called the Zucarellos "Uncle Joe" and "Aunt Norette." They called her "Gaba."

The Zucarellos treated Gabby like their own child. They made sure she went to school and did her homework, and they encouraged her to keep busy with sports and other activities she enjoyed.

Gabby loved the water, as her mother did, so the Zucarellos gave her swimming lessons. She also marched and twirled baton in a precision team called the Peanuts. In addition, the Zucarellos treated her to ballet lessons, which, as it turned out, Gabby absolutely hated.

The Zucarellos took Gabby everywhere. Together, they went on fishing and camping trips, to parks, and out for ice cream—just like any typical family. Gabby remembered her time on Long Island fondly. Aunt Norette, as Gabby wrote in her book *Big Girl in the Middle,* "saved my baby teeth. Joe showed me how to put someone in a full nelson [a wrestling move]."

In what seemed like a flash, the months with Uncle Joe and Aunt Norette turned into years.

"We gave her security when she needed it," explained Aunt Norette, "but she gave us so much more. She was our child."

Once in a while, Gabby's dad would take a plane from the islands to visit her on Long Island. But she was not destined to spend much time with either parent. When Gabby was just five, her father was killed in a plane crash. He was wearing a silver pendant when he died. Someone found the necklace and later presented it to Gabby. (When she grew older, Gabby had a picture of this cross tattooed on her ankle in tribute to her dad.)

Anyone who looked at long-legged Gabby could guess that she would grow up to be quite tall, just like her parents. At age seven, she already stood five feet tall, the size of many adult women. In fact, she was just two inches shorter than Aunt Norette. Once in a while when they saw Gabby from the back, some people mistook the little girl for a teacher!

Some of the other kids made fun of Gabby because of her height. They called her names like "Daddy Long Legs" and "Jolly Green Giant." In spite of all the teasing, she never slouched or wished she was shorter or smaller. The only thing Gabby ever wanted to change about herself was her hair. Since she grew up during a time when the wavy "winged" hair-styles were popular, she wished her hair was not so straight.

Gabby's mom had been gone for about four years now, and Gabby, Norette, and Joe had settled comfortably into their daily routine. Then one day, they were all surprised when the telephone rang. It was Terry. She was calling to say that she had remarried and had moved to the Caribbean island of Puerto Rico. She wanted Gabby to fly to the island and live with her and her new husband.

When Gabby heard the news, she stood on the sofa and cried. "Can't you get a lawyer?" the seven-year-old asked the Zucarellos.

Uncle Joe and Aunt Norette were also shocked and upset. They tried working with an attorney, so that Gabby could continue to live with them, but in the end were unsuccessful. Nothing could change the fact that Gabby was still legally Terry's daughter. Gabby would have to leave them and start a new life with her mom in Puerto Rico.

Saying goodbye was incredibly hard and sad for the Zucarellos. "It's a cliché, but I gotta say it," Norette remembered. "It was like losing an arm." Since Joe did not have a job in the area at that time, he and Norette closed up their house on Long Island and left to pursue work in Alaska. They took Gabby's furry friend, Daisy, with them.

Norette was especially heartbroken by the separation. Almost every day, she cried for the little girl that she had loved as her own. As it turned out, the Zucarellos did not get to talk to Gabby for an entire year.

If leaving was difficult for Aunt Norette and Uncle Joe, it was even harder for Gabby. Before she knew it, the seven-year-old was riding a plane bound for Puerto Rico, all by herself, not knowing what to expect about her mother, her new step-dad, or life in the islands.

The three eventually moved to St. Thomas, Virgin Islands. They lived in a neighborhood called Carrot Bay, facing the island's north shore. Their house was located along a ravine, a deep cliff that water had carved into the rock. If the weather was rainy, a small stream would

After several unexpected moves following the divorce of her parents, Gabrielle found herself living with her mother and stepfather on the Caribbean island of St. Thomas. Growing up here, however, wasn't always paradise for Gabby, who longed for stability and a sense of direction in her life.

sometimes form at the bottom of the cliff. Gabby enjoyed wandering through this area with her two new dogs, Lady and Felisse, who were mother and daughter.

Gabby quickly learned that her mother had not changed much. She was still the same free spirit and showed no interest in being a traditional mother.

Many kids would have loved the chance to skip school, and although Gabby had more than her share of chances, she never did. Instead, she behaved with remarkable responsibility. Each morning, she woke herself and dressed in the school's green plaid uniform. About an hour before they had to leave, Gabby would also start trying to wake up her mom, so she could drive her to school. She even made her coffee. After school, Gabby took a job folding T-shirts at a souvenir shop.

All this responsibility wore Gabby down and began to affect her health. When she was in the seventh grade, she started developing stomach problems. Her mom sent Gabby to see her Uncle Ted, a doctor who lived in California.

Uncle Ted said Gabby was suffering from an ulcer, a sort of "hole" that forms in the stomach's lining. He gave her medicine to help heal her ulcer. Over the next few weeks, Uncle Ted also spent a lot of time talking to his niece. Gabby needed the attention as much as—if not more than—the rest and medicine. By the time she returned home to the islands, Gabby was feeling much better.

Once Gabby reached junior high school, she was allowed to spend her summers visiting Uncle Joe and Aunt Norette back on Long Island. The three enjoyed happy, fun-filled weeks in the sun.

After the second summer with the Zucarellos, Gabby returned to St. Thomas before her mom did. Since she was not allowed to stay by herself, she had to live with a woman named Nanette until her mother came back. Gabby's stepfather had sent her $200 in case she needed anything, so she hid the money in her room. When Gabby returned to check it a few days later, it had disappeared—all $200.

A bathroom connected Gabby's room to the bedroom of another lady who lived with Nanette. Gabby walked into this woman's room and saw $200 lying on her dresser. She assumed it was hers and took it. When Nanette found out, she told Gabby to leave.

Gabby then stayed with her friend, Johann, and his mom. But since their house was much too tiny to accommodate three people, Gabby left once again. This time, she stayed with her mother's friend, also named Gabby, and her husband. In spite of all this turmoil, each day, even though she was only 13, she woke herself, got ready for school as usual, and caught a small dinghy that took her to the bus stop.

That year, she met Scott Skinner, who lived on St. Croix, a nearby island. He became her first boyfriend. Partly to get back at her mother, Gabby began rebelling. She snuck off to see Scott by taking airplanes to St. Croix. She also began drinking alcohol with friends. School, which she had usually made such an effort to attend, no longer interested her.

"I started getting into trouble," Gabby remembered. "I was drinking a lot, had no direction and wanted to drop out of school."

The island's environment did not make things any easier for her. There was no legal drinking age, and young kids acted as if they were adults.

"St. Thomas is such a raw place, very destructive," Gabby later explained in a *USA Today* interview. "It's very small, so there's not a lot of room for social niceties. It was very rough and all the kids are hard."

Around the same time, Terry separated from her second husband. She decided that she and Gabby would move, yet again—this time back to Long Island, New York. Although Gabby was sad about leaving her friends in the islands, she was looking forward to spending more time with the Zucarellos. She was also happy about seeing some of her friends again in New York.

School was set to begin in three days. Gabby was just starting to feel comfortable when Terry surprised her daughter with yet another shocking announcement.

"We're moving to Florida and you're going to school there," she said. Soon, mother and daughter were on the road once again. They settled in St. Petersburg, Florida to make another fresh start.

Terry decided Gabby should attend Keswick Christian School—a strict school where she hoped her daughter would learn better behavior. Unfortunately, Terry did not realize it was her own behavior and lack of responsibility, in part, that was making Gabby so miserable.

But despite the fact that her mom was not an ideal role model, Gabby developed some important talents during her childhood that would eventually guide her through difficult decisions in her adult life. She learned to be independent and to believe in herself. She learned to trust her instincts. She also learned the most important lesson—that no one could ever take these traits from her.

"I would take those 17 uncomfortable years any time in return for what I learned," Gabby later said, "because all the difficulties gave me some OK ideas as to how I wanted to live my life."

3

A TALL ORDER

Getting used to life at Keswick Christian Academy in Florida was a real adjustment for Gabby. The school's strict rules and prudish classmates were quite different from the lifestyle she had experienced in the islands. "Where I came from, 13-year-old girls behaved like 20-year-olds," she said. "There are no boundaries in the Virgin Islands, no legal drinking age, nowhere you can't go, nothing you can't do."

At Keswick, on the other hand, it seemed like there was nothing she was allowed to do. Gabby had to wear a modest uniform to school, and had to follow a rigid set of rules. Since she was so tall and the school had so few students, Gabby stood out even more than usual. In fact, only one boy at Keswick was taller than she was. Within her first few weeks at the Christian school, she got into a fight with three of the cheerleaders.

Around this time, Gabby's mom took her to visit a John Roberts Powers modeling agency in a local mall. At that time, most models were only 5'8" or 5'9". The staff took one look at Gabby and told her she was much too tall to model.

Wearing the Nike logo, Gabby shows her form during the 1996 Bud Light Tour. Using a regimen of tough workouts, sometimes five days a week, Gabby was able to get into peak condition.

Still, Gabby attended a few modeling classes and hired a photographer to take professional photos of her. A friend of her mom's, named Coral, said they should try another modeling agency. They followed Coral's advice and submitted Gabby's new photos.

One day later, that agency called Coral. They were impressed by Gabby's look and wanted to send her to Paris immediately for a modeling assignment. Gabby met the French modeling agent, named Philippe, at Coral's house. As soon as Terry saw Philippe, she had a bad feeling about him. She said that Gabby was not allowed to go to Paris.

Once again, Gabby had gotten her hopes up, and once again, she was disappointed. She was extremely angry at her mom. She thought that by not allowing her to go, Terry was just being mean and spiteful.

Coral kept in touch with Gabby. She still thought she should—and could—model professionally someday. As it turned out, however, Terry's gut instinct proved to be right. A few years later, an entertainment TV program ran a story about a few talent agents who had been behaving inappropriately with the young girls whom they were responsible for chaperoning. One of them was Philippe.

Playing sports turned out to be one acceptable way for Gabby to blow off steam and let loose. Even though she had never played basketball before, Gabby joined the team. She liked and respected her coach, Dean Soles.

The team ended the season by going to the state championship finals. Although Gabby also played a bit of volleyball, she stuck with basketball because she was better at it. She even went to a very prestigious basketball camp attended by the area's best basketball players. At that camp, Gabby decided that she did like basketball enough to play it all through college.

Around this time, Gabby developed a crush on a boy named Jeff Sandhoff. He was a year younger than Gabby and came from a very religious, conservative family. In fact, Jeff's father did not exactly trust the tall, sultry girl from the islands.

Jeff treated Gabby very well. They dated throughout their high school years, and Gabby even started going to church with Jeff on Sundays. Gabby was thrilled to finally be enjoying some stability. With new friends, sports, school, and the possibility of someday modeling, Gabby had finally found some balance in her life. But as was the case throughout most of her childhood, feeling too comfortable always proved to be dangerous.

The summer before her senior year, 1986, Gabby and her mom went to New York to visit Aunt Norette, Uncle Joe, and Gabby's grandmother. During their stay, Terry developed problems with her back and decided to stay in New York to see some doctors. She decided that Gabby would also be staying in New York with her and would not be returning to Keswick.

It was as if the rug had been whisked from beneath Gabby's feet. She felt crushed. The people at Keswick were upset, too. They had grown to love Gabby.

Keswick's principal, Tom Greener, called Terry and asked her if she would consider a proposition: Gabby could stay with him and his family for the rest of the term if Terry would let her return to Florida alone. Terry agreed, but since she and her second husband were in the process of divorcing, she made Gabby sign a contract promising she would not speak to her stepfather. Gabby kept her word.

4

YET ANOTHER FRESH START

Gabby moved in with the principal of Keswick Christian School and his wife and two children. She ended up staying with the Greeners for four months. Sometimes, she babysat for their kids. Occasionally Mr. Greener gave Gabby a ride to school on the back of his motorcycle.

After Gabby's favorite coach, Dean Soles, lost his job, she fell completely out of love with basketball. Instead, she set her sights on playing volleyball, which had begun to catch her interest. She even played club volleyball through the United States Volleyball Association after the school's season had ended. At the same time, she was doing well with her studies. Things seemed to be looking up again.

Gabby stood out from the other kids because of more than just her height. According to Mike Wells, Keswick's athletic director, Gabby was popular and independent. She " . . . seemed more mature than most of the kids," he remembered.

Like most high school seniors, Gabby began thinking seriously about which college she would attend. Her deci-

Focus is an important part of any pro athlete's success. Gabby's commitment to personal excellence, on and off the volleyball court, have helped make her one of today's most winning women.

sion finally came down to two institutions—the University of South Florida and the University of Tampa.

In her mind, Tampa had the edge for several reasons. She was going to study business, and the University in Tampa had a strong, well-respected business program. Gabby also liked the fact that Tampa's coach was also an islander from St. Croix, the island near St. Thomas and the place where her first boyfriend lived. By the time summer began, though, Gabby still had not made up her mind.

One weekend, Gabby was playing in the last volleyball tournament of the season at the University of Tampa. Her mom came to watch her play. When Florida State University's (FSU) coach, Cecile Reynaud, saw six-foot-tall Terry towering over the other women in the crowd, she immediately asked, "Where's the child connected with that woman?"

When Reynaud saw the child—Gabby—play volleyball, she saw that the girl had incredible talent. She offered Gabby the team's last scholarship within a matter of minutes.

Gabby immediately knew she liked Reynaud. She respected the fact that Reynaud was honest and did not mince words. Unlike coaches from other colleges, Reynaud did not try to "kiss up" to her to persuade her to come to FSU, and instead gave Gabby the space to make up her own mind.

It wasn't long before Gabby took a trip to visit FSU and learn more about its athletics and academics. By the end of the week, she signed her letter of intent, a sort of contract that stated she was planning to attend FSU. She was going to play on scholarship for the FSU Lady Seminoles. It turned out to be a wise decision that would open many doors for the young woman.

****

After struggling through her difficult first season, being named Most Improved Player, and landing some lucrative modeling jobs, Gabby returned to FSU her sophomore year with more confidence.

During the rest of her college career, Gabby split her time by spending six months—from August to January—at FSU training and the other six months—from January to August— on the road, modeling and earning money.

During the months that Gabby modeled, her teammates participated in a rigorous spring training session. The other girls resented the fact that Gabby did not have to train year-round, like they did. They were jealous of the fact that while they were running, sweating, and tending to their aching muscles, Gabby was doing photo shoots in cosmopolitan cities such as New York; Paris, France; and Milan, Italy. Gabby felt alone and disliked. It was diffi-cult for her to deal with.

"We all entered school together, 8 new play-ers out of 12 on the team, and they treated me like, 'Who in the hell do you think you are? You're only here half the year, you get all the attention . . .' "

One time, a teammate voiced her concerns at a team meeting. She said she did not think it was fair that Gabby got to play first string (the players who get to start the game—usually the best players) when she did not put in the same amount of hours as the rest of the girls. Now, it was painfully obvious to Gabby that they were jealous—both of her athletic ability and her beauty. Although she seemed to have everything a young woman could hope for, Gabby felt alienated and insecure. It would not be the last time she would have to deal with women who were jealous of her looks and ability.

There is a saying: "If it does not kill you it will make you stronger." As was the case with most hardships, Gabby learned to make the best of them. In the end, they always did seem to make her stronger.

According to Gabby, a girl who plays sports " . . . becomes a willing target for people to throw rocks at and she learns she can take it— one of the 10 life lessons. I've had people trash me . . . and because I'm a woman it hurts, but it doesn't kill me."

There is another saying: "perception rules reality." To the other girls in the team, it seemed as if Gabby was flying off, relaxing, and having a grand old time. They assumed that her life was easier than theirs.

But in reality, Gabby was working very hard and was behaving like an adult. Unlike most of her teammates, she did not have a real home or set of two parents to return to. She had to pay her bills, work, complete her studies, and practice. She had little time for the parties that most people associate with college life. In fact, she was behaving much more maturely than most college students. Unlike other women her age, she had no choice. She had no one to fall back on.

Although she was young, Gabby demonstrated another mature trait: integrity. She always placed volleyball first on her list of priorities. Once she turned down a $35,000 modeling job—more than many people earn in an entire year—because she did not want to miss an important volleyball game.

Despite the tension, the Lady Seminoles played extremely well. During Gabby's sophomore year, the team's finished with a record of 28 wins and 8 losses. Once again, they went to the NCAA Tournament.

During the first round game against Colorado State University, a volleyball hit Gabby hard in the face, putting her modeling career in jeopardy. Since her nose was bleeding, Coach Reynaud made her sit on the bench. Once she felt better, she told the coach she wanted to get back in the game.

"There was not any big concern for herself," Reynaud said. "She's really a team player. That's neat for any player, no matter what her face looks like."

It turned out to be a bad day. The Lady Seminoles lost and were knocked out of the tournament. But, all in all, it was a great year for Gabby. She had the team's best blocking record—171—and had racked up 350 kills. No wonder her teammates were so jealous. Even with just half the practice, Gabby's record spoke for itself; she was an athlete to be reckoned with.

That summer, Gabby switched to the Ford Modeling Agency, one of the world's best. She trotted the globe, modeling in Paris, Milan, Rome, Egypt, Mexico, and the Bahamas. Her pictures appeared in *Cosmopolitan, Harper's Bazaar, Elle,* and *In Fashion.*

Although the two fields seemed quite different, volleyball and modeling turned out to be exactly the right balance for Gabby. She knew she needed to do both to grow. And despite the fact that her photo was now gracing the covers of some of the world's most-read magazines, she did not take the modeling too seriously.

"I still knew that modeling would be important for me, just as I knew volleyball would. I

Known for her "kills" on the court, Gabby earned herself Most Valuable Offensive Player honors with her power and resilience. Here she spikes the ball during the 1996 Bud Light Tour in San Diego, California.

looked at both volleyball and fashion and I thought, 'Well, this is a little bit kooky, this mix, but we'll see what happens.' . . . I never went 'Ooooh, look at me, I'm a model.''

The next year, in 1989, the Lady Seminoles played even better. They ended their season with a record of 30 wins and 5 losses.

Unfortunately, they were knocked out on the first round of the NCAA Tournament.

Gabby played better, too. She racked up 212 blocks and 333 kills, a record that earned her a post on the All-Metro and American Volleyball Coaches All-South Teams. She also set a new FSU record with 69 solo blocks in a season.

The world was beginning to stand up and take notice of Gabby. The Dodge National Athletic Awards Committee named her the nation's Most Inspiring Collegiate Athlete. *Rolling Stone* magazine named her a "Wonder Woman of Sports." Of course, all of this recognition did not make her teammates feel any better. They were even more jealous of her success and beauty.

During Gabby's senior year, the team performed well again. The Lady Seminole's placed third on the Metro Conference, winning 25 games and losing 10. Gabby ended her college career with a record of 189 blocks—the team's best—and 328 kills. In her last NCAA tournament, FSU was knocked out again during the first round.

At one time, so much of Gabby's life seemed uncertain. But the independence and sense of responsibility that had been so trying during Gabby's childhood was now working to her advantage. In 1991, the girl who once thought about dropping out of high school earned a degree in communications. The star basketball player had evolved into one of the country's best volleyball players. The "Daddy Long Legs" who was told she was too tall to model was now gracing the covers of the world's top fashion magazines.

Gabby was an adult and in charge of her life. Each day was no longer just a matter of just survival. Gabby was succeeding—and liking it.

5

HITTING THE BEACH

After graduating from FSU, Gabby moved to sunny Miami, Florida. After all of her success in volleyball, college, and modeling, it seemed that the world was hers for the taking. She had planned on doing more modeling.

But, as was often the case in Gabby's life, things did not go as planned. Other than a few photo shoots for *Elle*, she was getting few modeling assignments. "I wasn't working, and suddenly, at 21, I had no money," she said. "No one wanted me anymore." Gabby knew from the start that the fashion world was fickle. Tastes change every few years, and established models are constantly replaced by fresh faces. Still, it did not make the rejection any easier.

While she was in Miami, Gabby met Barbara Bierman, a beach volleyball player. She talked Gabby into trying her hand at doubles beach volleyball.

Beach volleyball is much different than court volleyball. A doubles team only consists of two players, and Gabby was used to playing the position of middle blocker on an indoor, six-person team. She was good at this position, because she had spent more than four years practicing, perfecting her kills and blocks.

Gabrielle's beauty and athletic ability, coupled with hard work and training, have brought her to the peak of success as both a fashion model and pro volleyball player.

On the other hand, she did not know very much about setting the ball to another player, which was something that other players had always done for Gabby, or "digging" the ball—that is, stopping it from hitting the ground. Since these skills had always been her teammates' jobs, they were a mystery to Gabby. Now she would have to learn how to perfect each of them.

As if having to learn these new skills was not enough, playing outdoors in the sand added another challenge. The sand below a player's feet is uneven. Since it shifts, there is nothing firm from which a player can spring or jump. Basically, it slows a player down. (Sand, however, is much easier on an athlete's joints.) Toss in the uncertainly of the wind affecting the ball's spin and the glare of the sun in her eyes, and suddenly, everything about the game Gabby knew so well was different. It was, in a way, like starting from scratch.

Fortunately for Gabby, over the years, she had become very good at adjusting to and overcoming unexpected changes and challenges. She didn't waste much time worrying. Even though changing to beach doubles required a leap of faith, Gabby felt good about it. "Something I'm very fortunate to possess, more than my looks or even my athletic gifts, is the ability to trust what I know," she said. "I grew up trusting myself because I spent a childhood around adults I rarely trusted."

She got to work and started practicing with her new teammate. At first, it seemed as if Gabby's instincts had steered her wrong. Barbara and Gabby did not do well during their first Women's Professional Volleyball Association (WPVA) tournament in Puerto Rico in 1992. They lost both their first and second matches. But Barbara knew Gabby had talent and drive. She advised Gabby to move to California, where beach volleyball was gaining popularity.

With the help of another friend named Lily Stefano, Gabby scraped together enough money to move her things out west. Soon, she was headed across the country.

On her way to her new California home, Gabby and Barbara played in a tournament in Arizona and suffered a humiliating loss. At the same time, *People* magazine named Gabby one of 1992's "Most Beautiful People." She felt embarrassed because, in the article, she had referred to herself as a professional volleyball player and model. In reality, she did not feel that she was playing as well as a professional should. She was also no longer modeling. Once again, her whole world seemed to be spinning out of control.

As usual, though, Gabby wasted no time fretting. Just as she did as a novice player at FSU, Gabby knew the only way to improve her beach game was to practice more. She started training with a new friend named Holly McPeak. Although she worked hard, her instincts told her winning that season was out of the question. She decided to quit the WPVA and instead, concentrated on practicing her new skills.

Gabby knew in her heart that the position she played best was middle blocker. One day, a woman named Lisa Strand called her and asked her to play on a four-person team. Recognizing the opportunity—and the fact that she'd be able to play middle blocker again—she immediately agreed. Once again, Gabby's instincts led her correctly. She and her teammates finished their first tournament with a record of five wins and no losses.

It seemed that this type of volleyball was made for Gabby. "Four-person ball, a hybrid of indoor six-person court volleyball and doubles beach volleyball, is the perfect arena for Gabby's talents and strengths," said her FSU Coach Cecile Reynaud. It was not as structured as indoor, six-person ball, yet she did not have to re-learn a whole set of new skills, as she would with two-person ball. Four-person beach ball allowed Gabby to focus on what she did best—blocking and killing.

The proof came at the end of the season. League members voted Gabby their 1992 Most Valuable Player. Lady Foot Locker was so impressed by Gabby's performance during the 1992 season that they asked her to serve as their team's captain for the 1993 season. They even let her choose her own teammates.

Gabby, however, was not an experienced leader, and Lady Foot Locker's team did not fare so well, winning only two tournaments. It was, on the whole, however, a successful season for Gabby. She led the league racking up 27 kills and 53 blocks.

Little did Gabby know that representatives from Nike, the athletic shoe company, had been watching her play throughout the season. The fact that she was stunningly attractive and that she had modeled before also did not hurt. They gave her the opportunity to become the firm's first-ever female cross-training representative. In addition to posing for some photos and to doing some television spots, she would also get to serve as the Nike's team captain and choose her own teammates for the next year's season. They would also pay her for training and competing in the various tournaments and would give her free sneakers, athletic clothing, and equipment. With so many potential benefits, the Nike deal was an offer Gabby could not refuse.

But not everyone at Nike was thrilled about hiring Gabby. Some of the company's marketing people thought she was too feminine to be a spokesperson for an athletic shoe manufacturer.

Nike finally decided to solve this "problem" by starring Gabby in a funny TV commercial called "Gabbing with Gabby." In the commercial, they essentially tried to redefine femininity. They wanted to show that, although Gabby was what most people would consider a beautiful woman—a professional model with classic features and grace—she was also a talented, aggressive athlete.

In the commercial, Gabby strolled around wearing a tank top and swimsuit bottom. She gave the TV audience "advice" about dieting, make up, and the modeling life. These "girly girl" shots were interrupted by film showing Gabby sweating, working out, and playing aggressive volleyball. Even though the commercial was funny, it was, in a sense, an almost perfect short biography of Gabby. Although she had many talents, she was most noticed for her beauty and athletic ability. Even though they seemed like opposites, Gabby was able to use them both to her advantage.

The commercial also exploded stereotypes (an oversimplified way of looking at people) on both sides of Gabby's professions. Athletes, for example, had a hard time believing that a pretty, delicate-looking model could actually play an aggressive, intelligent game of volleyball.

And other models had a difficult time understanding how or why a model would want to waste her time and risk marring her looks by playing sports.

Unlike many models, Gabby ate whatever she wanted. Of course, she was conscious of keeping a healthy diet, in order to maintain her top athletic performance, but she never denied herself any foods she craved.

"I can eat anything I want and burn it," she said. " . . . I go back and forth. This morning, I ate egg whites and brown rice; if I feel like a cheeseburger, then I'll eat a cheeseburger. But I'm also willing to work hard."

Besides gearing up for the 1994 volleyball season, Gabby also did some photo shoots for various Nike ads and completed a few interviews in magazines and newspapers. She also appeared on TV shows such as ABC's "Primetime Live." MTV eventually hired her to serve as a correspondent for *MTV Sports*, a show that featured and profiled athletes. Gabby even helped design a new sneaker called the Air Trainer Set. She was becoming a familiar American face.

Still, in spite of her new-found fame, Gabby's strong work ethic had not changed. Her volleyball game remained most important to her. She practiced hard and worked out religiously.

While it can be difficult to be an ugly duckling, beauty and talent can also come with their own share of problems. Sometimes, it is more difficult to manage success than it is to handle failure. Just like at FSU, Gabby's new Nike team members resented her for all of the attention she was getting. They were jealous of her beauty, her fame, and her athletic ability.

Although switching from hard-court to beach volleyball proved tricky for Gabby, she adapted her technique to meet the challenge.

By this time, though, Gabby had had enough practice dealing with jealous women. She knew that she worked just as hard, if not harder, than they did. She felt that she did not need to prove to them that she was committed to the team. Instead, she worked hard on her game. During the season, as usual, she pushed aside all of her other commitments in order to concentrate completely on her volleyball game.

That season, Team Nike only won 3 out of 12 tournaments. But Gabby set a league record by racking up 454 total kill attempts—about 12 in each game. The league named her the

Offensive Player of the Year. Again, some players tried to tone down the fact that Gabby had won the award by saying that she had more sets than anyone. Gabby was not bothered. Jealous teammates were becoming so common that they just did not faze her anymore. She had bigger fish to fry.

Many different companies offered Gabby projects. In addition to doing more modeling for Nike, *Elle* magazine asked Gabby to be a contributing fitness editor. The NBA's "Inside Stuff" show also hired her to work as a sports commentator.

Despite all these commitments, Gabby's main focus was to practice and to work out. At least five mornings a week, sometime more often, she completed two-hour training sessions at Gold's Gym in Venice, California. The workouts were more demanding than Gabby ever could have guessed, but as always, she rose to meet the challenge.

"I threw up the first time I did this workout," she said in an interview in *Sport* magazine. "You finish and you're tired, drenched. Forget physical, it's mentally grinding."

Gabby's reward for all this grueling effort was a better-oiled, more dynamic "machine"— her body. The workouts, which included weight training, helped her get into tip-top shape. She knew that achieving this superior level of physical fitness would give her a competitive edge over the many talented volleyball players she was about to face during the 1995 season. Gabby had proved that hard work was one thing she did not shy away from. She took her responsibility to the Nike team, and to herself, quite seriously.

And as if these training sessions were not difficult enough, each afternoon Gabby hit the beach to perfect her volleyball game. She played and did drills for about two hours. After all that she had achieved, the stakes were high. She did not want to blow it by failing to practice enough.

Her coach, Gary Sato, talked about her untiring dedication. "She is committed to being the best she can be. I've heard her say that her good looks she didn't earn. This takes a lot of work."

For Gabby, these workouts also gave her a personal payoff. "I like the idea of the working hard thing," she wrote in her book, *Big Girl in the Middle*. "When I come out of the gym . . . I feel worthy of living and breathing and walking around—and absolutely, enhancement of athletic performance. When I am doing the circuit, I don't care about anything besides becoming a better athlete. The circuit is too hard. Nothing else could get me there."

So, by the time the 1995 season opened, she was ready to face her opponents.

6

DRIVING AMBITION

As usual, Gabby put all of her other activities and commitments on hold so she could focus completely on volleyball during the season. Her strenuous workouts and intense practice sessions paid off, to the tune of 482 kills. Once again, she was also named the Offensive Player of the Year. Her team, on the other hand, did not fare so well. Nike only won 2 of 12 tournaments, putting a damper on Gabby's personal victories.

When the season ended, Gabby found a new job to keep her busy. Executives at MTV asked her to host a new program called *The Extremists*. This show profiled athletes who participated in risky or "extreme" sports. Gabby even got to try some of these offbeat, and sometimes dangerous, activities. She surfed, boxed, kayaked, and even went sky–diving. (Later, she jokingly called this job her "crash test dummies" phase). Little did Gabby guess that this show would lead her to take one of the biggest risks of her life— allowing herself to fall in love.

Gabby and husband Laird Hamilton take a break from sports to enjoy a night on the town in New York City.

While filming MTV's *Extreme Sports* on location in Hawaii, Gabby met top surfer Laird Hamilton. During the 1996 season, a romance bloomed between the two athletes. The pair married in 1997.

Gabby was filming several episodes of the show in Hawaii. One day, while working on a show about strap surfing on the exotic island of Maui, she met Laird Hamilton, one of the world's top surfers. Gabby knew immediately that she was attracted to him.

Laird was as tall as Gabby—6 feet, 3 inches. Like her, his hair was bleached blond from spending so much time in the sun. And like Gabby, Laird loved to take risks and face challenges. He had, for example, paddled across the English Channel. He had been injured so many times that he had racked up an impressive "record" of more than 1,000 stitches.

When she returned home to California, she missed Laird—even though she had only spent a short time with him. Like a lovesick schoolgirl, she could not stop thinking about him.

"Can we just eat lunch with Laird? Please?" she asked her girlfriend one afternoon. Gabby put a VCR tape of the surfer on pause, so she could look at it while she and her friend had lunch. It was not at all like Gabby to be so sentimental.

Laird also shared a few eerie similarities with Gabby's father. Like Eduardo Reece, Laird was a handsome island man, born and raised on the Hawaiian island of Kauai. An independent person, he deeply respected the ocean and nature.

Gabby was used to being in charge. By fostering a "take control" attitude, she found that it was easier to achieve her goals and to avoid getting hurt. But after her adventure in Hawaii, she learned that, sometimes, life calls the shots. There are many situations in life—most, in fact—over which people have no control. She

found that surrendering to this "wave" sometimes yield incredible rewards. Soon, Gabby
and Laird were dating, and spending more and
more time together.

By the time the 1996 season began, the two
athletes became inseparable. Laird went to all
of Gabby's volleyball tournaments to offer
encouragement and support. Many more familiar faces came to cheer Gabby on during the
season. Aunt Norette and Uncle Joe, who now
lived in Phoenix, Arizona, came to watch a few
matches, as did Gabby's manager, Jane
Kachmer. A writer named Karen Karbo, who
was working with Gabby on her book, *Big Girl
in the Middle,* also attended most of the games.
Even her mom Terry stopped by.

As it turned out, Gabby needed all the support she could get. The team was not playing
well. After much soul-searching, she realized
that some of the other team members were not
working out and were bogging down the rest of
the team. She was faced with a difficult decision. Although it was hard for her, Gabby fired
her setter, Liane Sato. She also replaced her
coach of three years, Gary Sato (Liane's broth-
er), with Charlie Brand.

During practice, the new team, which consisted of Jen Meredith at setter, Katie Haller at
outside hitter, Kim Crawford at outside, and
Gabby in the middle, seemed more promising.
After a few matches, Gabby knew that she also
had to cut Kim Crawford, who was too inexperi-
enced and emotional. She replaced Kim with
Julie Bremner.

But Gabby still was not happy with the team
she had chosen. A few weeks later, she fired

Katie Haller and replaced her with a tough player, Christine "The Rocket" Romero. To someone watching, it seemed as if Gabby was playing chess by moving her players.

Even with all the roster changes and grueling practice session, Nike's team suffered from a particularly disappointing season. They won only one of the ten tournaments in which they competed. Although Gabby led the league with 547 kills, it did not make her feel any better about the difficult year or her bad decisions. Although she certainly had many talents, it was obvious that choosing a team was not among them.

The next year, the beach volleyball's tour directors decided to choose their own team members. Nike's 1997 lineup consisted of Gabby, Stephanie Cox, Katy Eldridge, and Jenny Johnson. The chemistry between these four women was much better. The team won four straight tournaments and finished the season in second place. For the first time in four years, Gabby did not lead the league in kills, but she still finished in an impressive third place.

All in all, that year was a good one for Gabby. She and Laird got married. *Women's Sports and Fitness Magazine* placed Gabby's photo on the cover and aptly named her one of "The 20 Most Influential Women in Sports." She definitely deserved this honor, since she had dissolved the boundaries between beauty and athleticism. She had proven to both the sports world and the fashion that the two ideals do not have to exist separately.

Always one to shake things up a bit, Gabby decided to give two-person volleyball another try in 1999. But some things never change. As was the case back when she first played doubles with Barbara Bierman, she did not fare well. Gabby's strong body was still too powerful for this two-person game. Doubles requires speed and agility while Gabby's strengths lie more in her brute force.

In late 1999, life threw Gabby another curve ball. David Lee, an ex-professional golfer and talent scout, called Gabby to tell her about Cravity Golf. This training program teaches professional athletes how to become professional golfers. Although Gabby had played golf before, she certainly did not consider herself pro material. And putting the ball in frumpy golf clothing was not exactly her favorite pastime.

"I wasn't very good, to put it mildly," she said. "I never understood the intense passion people have for such a boring activity. It's not even a sport; it's a game."

But just as she always had done, Gabby listened to her gut. Never one to turn down an opportunity—especially an unconventional one—Gabby decided to give golf a swing. She met with Lee for her first training session on her 30th birthday, January 6, 2000.

In some ways, learning to play professional golf was like "un-learning" all the skills Gabby needed to play volleyball well. Although her instinct was to use all of her power to drive the golf ball, for example, Lee instead taught her to relax. He told her to visualize "throwing the ball toward the hole." Lee thought that that if

Gabby trained for five days a week for a year, she would have a shot at the Ladies Pro Golf Association (LPGA) tour.

As she perfected her golf swing with practice, later switching to the Butch Harmon School for Golf in Las Vegas, Nevada, Gabby gained confidence and skill. Although she was not exactly crazy about the idea at first, golf grew on Gabby as she played more.

"We all have personal missions in life," she once said. "Mine is not so different from most people's—finding and maintaining peace of mind. The catch is that for me that means constantly challenging myself. If I don't have some sort of personal challenge every day, I'm a nightmare to live with." While she knew that she would still be able to play a few more years of

Never one to shy away from a challenge, Gabby has begun to explore her other athletic talents. Although learning golf meant "un-learning" some of her volleyball skills, she has shown her ability to succeed on the green.

Equally talented on the green as on the volleyball court, Gabby looks forward to a career in pro golf after her years of volleyball are behind her.

beach volleyball, she liked the idea that golf could extend her "shelf life" as an athlete. "It could also give me another chance to dream . . . " she said. "I enjoy the thrill of learning a new skill and the excitement of the unknown. It's not about becoming a great golfer; it's about not limiting myself."

Gabby's long training hours on the green have has paid off. The woman who considered herself a poor golfer can now drive a golf ball about 280 yards. She is scheduled to compete in the LPGA in either 2001 or 2002.

In true Gabby fashion, she is spinning quite a few plates at once. She still occasionally models for high–profile magazines. Gabby is also planning to share her years of experience in health and fitness with others through a new book. In the future, she might also complete some health and fitness videos.

Gabby also makes occasional television appearances. Lifetime TV featured her biography on their show *Intimate Portrait*. A video game firm immortalized Gabby's playing technique in a video game called *Power Spike Pro Beach Volleyball*. Fans can play as Gabby's character or compete against her video "twin."

An important by-product of all of Gabby's accomplishments is the fact that she has become an inspiring role model for young women—both athletes and non-athletes alike. She is strong yet vulnerable, comfortable with her body, educated, and opinionated.

"If I could represent one thing to women, it would be to be a woman who doesn't necessarily choose to be one thing," she says. " . . . I

would like to represent someone who, regard-
less of the degree of support, listens to her own
voice instead of trying to conform to a bunch of
societal rules that change every five or ten
years anyway."

STATISTICS

Two-Person Volleyball

Year	Place	Tournament
1999	17th	FIVB Beach Volleyball Tour, Marseille, France
	5th	AVP Grand Slam Event, Muskegon, MI
	3rd	AVP Grand Slam Event, Chicago, IL
	17th	FIVB Beach Volleyball Tour, Toronto, Canada
	3rd	Olympic Challenge Series, Virginia Beach, VA
	5th	Olympic Challenge Series, Huntington Beach, Ca
	17th	FIVB Beach Volleyball Tour, Acapulco, Mexico
	7th	AVP Grand Slam Event, Hermosa Beach, CA
	5th	AVP Grand Slam Event, Clearwater, FL
1998	2nd	Labatt's Pro National Tour, Ontario, Canada
1997	1st	World Championships of Beach Volleyball, Los Angeles, CA

Four-Person Volleyball

Year	Wins	Tournament	Team
1997	4	Newport, RI; Chicago, IL	Nike (captain)
1996	0		Nike (captain)
1995	2	St. Paul, MN; Newport, RI	Nike (captain)
1994	3	Turtle Bay, HI; Manhattan Beach, CA; Boston, MA	Nike (captain)
1993	2	Seal Beach, CA; Tampa, FL	Lady Foot Locker (captain)

Career Highlights

1993–1996	Lead league in kills
1993	Lead league in blocks
1994	Set league record for kills per match (11.9), kills in a tournament (63), and total attempts in a tournament (173); named Offensive Player of the Year
1996	Set league record for kills in a season (547)
1997	Inducted into the Florida State University Athletic Hall of Fame

CHRONOLOGY

1970	Gabrielle Reece is born in LaJolla, California on January 6.
1973	Gabby's mother sends her to live with Joe and Norette Zucarello on Long Island, New York.
1975	Eduardo Reece, Gabby's father, dies in a plane crash.
1977	Gabby returns to St. Thomas to live with her mother and new stepfather.
1985	Moves to Florida and attends Keswick Christian School. Starts playing basketball and tries volleyball.
1987	Enters FSU on a scholarship. Voted the team's Most Improved Player; begins modeling.
1988	Leads FSU's team in blocks (171) and kills (350). Modeling photos appear in *Cosmopolitan*, *Harper's Bazaar*, *Elle*, and *In Fashion*.
1989	Racks up 212 blocks and 333 kills; is named to the All-Metro and American Volleyball Coaches All-South Teams. Sets a new FSU record with 69 solo blocks in a season. The Dodge National Athletic Awards Committee names her the nation's Most Inspiring Collegiate Athlete. *Rolling Stone* magazine names her a "Wonder Woman of Sports."
1990	Leads the team with 189 blocks and 328 kills. Graduates from college.
1992	Begins playing beach doubles volleyball. Is named one of *People* magazine's "Most Beautiful People." Switches to four-person volleyball and is named captain of Lady Foot Locker's Team. Leads league in blocks and kills.

1994	Signs a contract to represent Nike. Serves as team captain. Leads league in kills; named Offensive Player of the Year; serves as a correspondent for *MTV Sports*.
1995	Leads league in kills; named Offensive Player of the Year.
1996	Leads league in kills; hired to host MTV's *The Extremists*.
1997	Marries Laird Hamilton; co-authors a book, *Big Girl in the Middle*.
2000	Begins training to become a professional golfer.

FURTHER READING

Morgan, Teri. *Gabrielle Reece: Volleyball's Model Athlete.* Minneapolis: Lerner, 1999.

Reece, Gabrielle, and Karen Karbo. *Big Girl in the Middle.* New York: Crown, 1997.

Kiraly, Karch. *Karch Kiraly's Championship Volleyball.* New York: Fireside, 1996.

Heywood, Leslie. *Pretty Good for a Girl.* The Free Press, 1998.

Oleksak, Michael. *The Basic Elements of the Game.* Lincolnwood, Illinois: NTC Publishing Group, 1996.

INDEX

ABOUT THE AUTHOR

A freelance writer, DYNISE BALCAVAGE is also the author of six other books including *Ludwig van Beethoven*, *Steroids*, *The Great Chicago Fire*, and *The Federal Bureau of Investigation*. Additionally, Balcavage has written many magazine articles, essays, poems, short stories, and book reviews. She occasionally does poetry readings and teaches writing classes in the Philadelphia area.

Balcavage has visited many foreign lands including Jordan, Israel, Morocco, Turkey and has spent a great deal of time in Europe, especially in France. She earned a B.F.A. in visual arts from Kutztown University and an M.A. in English from Beaver College. She lives in Philadelphia with her husband, cat, and two birds.

HANNAH STORM, NBC Sports play-by-play announcer, reporter, and studio host, made her debut in 1992 at Wimbledon during the All England Tennis Championships. Shortly thereafter, she was paired with Jim Lampley to cohost the Olympic Show for the 1992 Olympic Games in Barcelona. Later that year, Storm was named cohost of *Notre Dame Saturday*, NBC's college football pregame show. Adding to her repertoire, Storm became a reporter for the 1994 Major League All-Star Game and the pregame host for the 1995, 1997, and 1999 World Series. Storm's success as host of *NBA Showtime* during the 1997–98 season won her the role as studio host for the inaugural season of the Women's National Basketball Association in 1998.

In 1996, Storm was selected as NBC's host for the Summer Olympics in Atlanta, and she has been named as host for both the 2000 Summer Olympics in Sydney and the 2002 Winter Olympics in Salt Lake City. Storm received a Gracie Allen Award for Outstanding Personal Achievement, which was presented by the American Women in Radio and Television Foundation (AWRTF), for her coverage of the 1999 NBA Finals and 1999 World Series. She has been married to NBC Sports broadcaster Dan Hicks since 1994. They have two daughters.